"CONFLICT!

but none of us can. *Pebbles in My Shoe* tackles a tough topic beautifully. Linda outlines a simple and very effective way to address and resolve conflict so that relationships can flourish and individuals can find more peace. Well done!"

—Jeff Lautt, President, POET, LLC

"One of the great struggles in life is learning to navigate conflict. We've all been there, flooded by emotion, hoping, wanting, believing there's answers. Well, there is. *Pebbles in My Shoe* is a proven, step-by-step success manual. I wish I would have had it 20 years ago."

—Dr. Keith Loy, Lead Pastor,
Celebrate Community Church

"The tools introduced by Linda Outka provide a road map to navigating through conflict. With Linda's coaching, I've applied these principles to leading my company and they've moved our culture forward."

—Sean Coffman, Entrepreneur,
Founder and CEO, Carsforsale.com

"I attribute much of the success our company has had to a culture built on shared values. Those values are integrity, openness, respect for people and accountability. To actually get people to embrace a culture takes more than just tag lines, it requires serious skill building. In my view there is nothing more challenging than creating an environment that embraces effective conflict resolution. It is a skill that is critical to success, but difficult to implement. Linda Outka has developed strategies that are tangible and effective in exploring this critical component of business and personal success."

—Michael Masterson, Retired CEO,
Sammons Enterprises

PEBBLES

in

MY SHOE

PEBBLES

in

MY SHOE

Three Steps to Breaking through Interpersonal Conflict

LINDA P. OUTKA

Foreword by Kary Oberbrunner

Author of Elixir Project, Day Job to Dream Job,
The Deeper Path & Your Secret Name

Published by Author Academy Elite
P.O. Box 43, Powell, OH 43035
www.AuthorAcademyElite.com

Paperback ISBN-13: 978-1-943526-87-1
Hardback ISBN-13: 978-1-943526-86-4

Library of Congress Control Number: 2016914646

To Troy, my soulmate.
Thank you for always believing in me.
To Caitlin, Mitchell and Ian.
You give me immeasurable joy.

CONTENTS

Step 1—Base Camp: The Preparation

Step 2—Ascent: The Conversation

Step 3—Summit: The Gratification

FOREWORD

BY KARY OBERBRUNNER

When there's more than one person in a room, there's potential for conflict. Differing opinions, diverse personalities and varied expertise are all parts of the formula that make disagreements a common occurrence. Although conflict can derail a team or a family—it can also become the catalyst for more fulfilling relationships.

The distinction depends on whether you work *around* the conflict or *through* it. At times it may seem easier to avoid the issue and the person we're in conflict with. But unfortunately, the problem doesn't go away by simply ignoring it.

Author Linda Outka is uniquely qualified to help you navigate the journey to breaking through the conflict that drains your energy and diffuses your focus. The path may seem elusive, but Linda's three-step plan is proven to resolve conflicts and restore relationships.

Pebbles in my Shoe is a bold journey down a proven path. Linda has been helping people work through conflict for more than 20 years and it's her passion to create a safe space for people to achieve breakthroughs in interpersonal relationships.

I have been coaching Linda for over five years. No joke—the first time I met her, I found her heart for conflict resolution infectious. To this day I've never met anyone more committed to helping individuals and organizations turn potentially devastating situations into turning points for internal and external change.

Linda has a God-given gift that she shares with us through this book that I now consider her OPUS. You and your relationships will benefit from this master coach and teacher. But like anything in life, knowledge alone won't renew your relationships. Wisdom will only be embodied as you practice and apply these principles in your everyday life.

If you're ready to get "pebble-free" personally and professionally, keep reading. It's your time for a breakthrough solution.

Kary Oberbrunner
Author of *ELIXIR Project*, *Day Job to Dream Job*, *The Deeper Path* and *Your Secret Name*

ACKNOWLEDGMENTS

I want to thank my business coach, Kary Oberbrunner. When Kary and I met at the John Maxwell certification for coaches, speakers and trainers, the first words out of his mouth were, "Have you ever thought about writing a book?" Five years later, not only has Kary coached me through the process of writing a book, but he has also guided me through the steps of launching my coaching and speaking business, Breakthrough Solutions, Inc. Kary has consistently developed excellent resources that have added rich tools to my toolbox. When I became certified as a coach and facilitator for *Your Secret Name* and *The Deeper Path*, the insights I was able to offer in workshops and coaching sessions grew exponentially.

I have been blessed to have three key prayer partners and front-row supporters: my mom, Anita Pelzer; my sister, Deb Brown; and my dear friend, Megan Jerke. These three gave me prayer cover for each writing session. Also, thanks to the many others who gave me prayer support and encouragement.

Thank you to the eight individuals who spent countless hours helping me edit the book. I'm indebted to my husband and chief editor, Troy Outka; my mom, Anita Pelzer; my sister, Deb Brown; my mentor, Brian Rohr; and my dear friends Lori DeWitt, Megan Jerke, Kelli Langfitt and Leann Ortman.

Thank you to my sister-in-law, Terri Carlson, for the inspiration behind the title, *Pebbles in My Shoe*, and for her support and encouragement.

Above all, I am grateful to my Lord and Savior, Jesus Christ. I give him all the glory.

INTRODUCTION

PEBBLES: THE MOTIVATION

I *used* to like my job. That is until my boss, Jack, suddenly changed.

Jack started to ask me for weekly reports itemizing everything I did that week. Our usual easy conversational style had become strangely strained. I noticed Jack wasn't coming into my office as much as he used to for casual chats. Something had changed in our relationship, and I couldn't put my finger on it. It felt like he didn't trust me and I had no idea why. Jack's normal laissez-faire management style had transitioned into a micromanagement style, and it was sucking the life out of me.

I knew we needed to talk, but I also knew I needed to wait until the right moment to ask Jack about the change in our working relationship. To keep him from getting defensive, I realized I would have to start with a curious question. I'd been talking to my steering wheel on the way to work, practicing the questions I could ask. I had an anxious feeling in the pit of my stomach, wondering if this would be the day I would clear the air with Jack. I kind of hoped so, yet I didn't mind procrastinating one more day. What if the conversation didn't go well?

That afternoon I was in Jack's office, and he seemed to be in an unusually good mood. We talked about a number of subjects and then there was a lull in the conversation. I decided to take the plunge. "Jack, can I ask you a question?" I started tentatively.

"Sure," he responded.

I began slowly, measuring my words carefully. "I've noticed that you're wanting more and more reports from me," I started, trying to remember what I had practiced saying to my steering wheel that morning. "And we're spending less time face-to-face planning. Is that meeting your needs? I mean—is that working for you?"

"Ah, no not really," Jack admitted. "I'm not sure what I really want. But no, those reports really aren't working for me."

"Can I ask another question?" I asked.

"Yeah, sure," Jack replied.

I continued, trying to muster up the courage to verbalize the deeper question that was in my gut. "It seems like our working relationship has really changed in the past couple of months. I feel like you don't trust me as much as you used to. Is there something I've done that triggered that change?"

I looked over at Jack. He paused.

His pause was evidence enough. This strain in our relationship wasn't just in my imagination.

"Yes—there is something," Jack said slowly, then stopped.

"Please go on," I encouraged. "I want to know."

Jack started again. "Do you remember when we had our all-employee meeting two months ago, and Allan (the head of our organization) came from California to give the keynote address? One of the main points of his talk was on culture, and he highlighted the culture-shaping workshops you were going to be facilitating."

"Yes," I said, "I remember that."

"Well, afterward," Jack continued, "when you came up to the stage to introduce yourself to Allan, I was standing within hearing distance. I was hoping you would let him know you reported to me, and I was the person who gave you the opportunity to facilitate those workshops. Not only did you fail to mention me to Allan, but you didn't even acknowledge my presence when you passed by. It made me wonder if you intended to be a rising star who took all the credit for yourself."

I felt like I had been punched in the stomach.

"Wow. I can see how you felt that way," I managed to choke out. "And I am so sorry."

There was a pregnant pause. I felt the atmosphere in the room shift. The ice in our relationship began to melt.

"Would you be open to hearing about what was going on for me that afternoon?" I asked.

"Sure," Jack responded.

I collected my thoughts and began slowly. "I had slipped into the all-employee meeting just before they closed the doors so I climbed the steps to the back of the auditorium, hoping to be rather invisible. The meeting got underway, and Allan was introduced as the keynote speaker. Unexpectedly, Allan mentioned the culture workshops that were going to be launched and that I was one of the facilitators. I was taken by surprise. I wasn't prepared for that announcement. Since I had never met Allan before, I knew I should probably introduce myself to him afterward because I may not get another opportunity. I instantly became self-conscious. I hadn't dressed professionally that day and frankly, I was having a bad hair day. But when the meeting ended, I made my way down to the stage and mustered up enough courage to wait in line, trying to think of something intelligent to say after 'Hello, my name is Linda Outka.'

"I was flushed and nervous when I got to the front of the line. I held out my hand and introduced myself, hoping my insecurity wasn't too obvious. After the interaction, I quickly turned to walk away. I saw you off to the side, but you had already looked away before I could wave. I'm so sorry I didn't acknowledge you or let Allan know about our connection. Will you forgive me?"

Jack looked at the table, then back at me. It seemed like the pause lasted forever.

"Not a problem," Jack replied sincerely.

I was relieved. From that day forward, our working relationship and friendship began to grow. Over the years that followed, Jack and I developed a trust that far surpassed the quality of our relationship even prior to this intense breakthrough conversation. We talked about family. We talked about faith. We even talked about politics. We shared life experiences.

A few years later, Jack was tragically killed in a car accident. When I first heard the news, I was shocked. He was a good man who would be sorely missed. Then I began to reflect on our relationship. During the nine years I had reported to him, we had many deep conversations. Fortunately, my reflections were filled with fond memories. If Jack and I had not cleared the air several years before, my reflections would have quickly turned into regret. Reconciliation is powerful and can last for an eternity.

How We Accumulate Pebbles

We don't wake up in the morning with the intention of offending a family member, a co-worker or the person behind the lunch counter that day. But everyday conversations can quickly go awry without warning, and someone gets offended. It happens to me, and I'll bet it happens to you too.

So what do you do with these conversations when you've been offended? If you react in the moment, it's usually not your most stellar performance. If you go silent, you can end up seething later. If you don't deal with your feeling of offense in a productive manner, each hurt can become a pebble in your shoe.

Do you remember the last time you got a pebble in your shoe? How long did it take you to stop and remove it? If you would have left it there, how often would you have thought about it? Eventually, it would have created a wound.

Similarly, the hurts in our relationships are distracting. We think about the hurt when we're in the same room with the person who offended us. We think about it when we're alone with our own thoughts. It drains our energy. It wounds our spirit.

So why do we avoid removing a relational pebble from our shoe? Why do we choose to live with the pain instead?

In talking with people who have lived with a strained relationship for years or even decades, they say they would have addressed it with the person if they had thought it would do any good.

Or they don't know where to start. Or they tried, and the conversation was a train wreck.

This book is for readers who would like to remove the pebbles from their shoes, but don't know where to start. It's for those who feel they've reached a dead end with what they've tried in the past.

I've used the steps in this book as a model for conflict resolution for more than 20 years, both personally and professionally. The principles that we will discuss have worked with interpersonal conflicts between co-workers, neighbors, friends, couples, parents and children. Relationships are not a science, so unfortunately, formulas don't work. But if you apply the concepts outlined in this book, you will experience more enriched relationships. We cannot change another person, but when *we* change, the relationship changes. And that's the key. We can only start with ourselves.

In our journey toward conflict resolution, mountain climbing may be a helpful metaphor. Like a climber uses a base camp to prepare, adjust to altitude changes, pack and plan, conflict resolution needs a base camp too. When we prepare ourselves through reflection and soul searching, we will proceed carefully. In order to avoid a "here goes nothing" or "the truth hurts" approach to confrontation, we need a plan. We need a roadmap. Preparation, or **Base Camp,** is critical to effective conflict resolution.

The second step for removing a pebble in our shoe is the conversation itself, which we'll call the **Ascent.** Like climbing a mountain, conflict resolution conversations require courage and stamina. The dialogue will likely bring unexpected twists and turns. To make the Ascent successful, we will talk about how to start the conversation and how to keep the conversation from getting defensive. We will discuss how to effectively use examples to create clarity and understanding. We will explore how to come to an agreement that is mutually beneficial.

The third and final step is gratification: the **Summit.** The reward for the mountain climber is the sense of accomplishment and the view at the top. The reward for one who resolves a conflict is a new perspective and a more fulfilling relationship. Both parties who ascended the mountain together and reached the Summit have a new view. They have gained understanding because they have authentically listened to each other's stories. The conversation has enlightened both people and as a result, they are changed. A conversation of this caliber is about aha moments, growth and learning. The relationship goes deeper. When you take a pebble out of your shoe, you walk with more freedom. You get more of what you want and less of what you don't want.

In more than 20 years of being a business coach, I have repeatedly witnessed how conflicts zap creativity, productivity and joy. I have seen people walk away from careers, churches, friendships and marriages because they were unable to resolve their interpersonal issues. It's tragic and unnecessary.

I have been honored to witness what happens when a person has the courage to address an issue directly with the one she's in conflict with. When she conquers her fears and has the conversation, she walks away with greater confidence.

The stories you will read in the pages of this book are inspired by personal experiences and coaching conversations I've had. Names and details of the situations have been changed to create anonymity and protect confidentiality. Even though I've taken editorial license, the principles we can learn from the conversations remain intact.

I have been facilitating the resolution of conflict in various contexts for more than 20 years, and the model contained in these pages has evolved through this work. I am indebted to Susan Scott and the confrontation model she presents in her book *Fierce Conversations*. I was certified as a facilitator with Fierce Conversations three years ago, and the principles Scott outlines in both her book and her workshops helped refine my model of conflict resolution.[1]

So whether you'd like new tools to resolve a conflict for yourself or if you need resources to help coach someone you care about, this book will give you the roadmap.

Let's begin our journey.

STEP 1

BASE CAMP: THE PREPARATION

CHAPTER 1

WHAT'S AT STAKE?

I walked into Jackie's office for our regular coaching session. She looked stressed. Jackie worked for a large manufacturing company, and I knew she was under a great deal of pressure to accomplish her business goals that quarter. But the look on her face indicated this was a different kind of stress.

When I asked her what she'd like to focus on in our coaching session, she told me she was having quite a bit of tension with her colleague Aaron. Jackie and Aaron had worked together for five years. They were part of a management team that was tight. They spent time outside of work together and were part of one of the most cohesive teams I've worked with. When the stress from their jobs was high, they had each other's backs. But things had shifted in the past two weeks.

Two weeks ago, Jackie and Aaron were in a monthly meeting where they had been questioned by the president of the company as to why production was slow and customers were complaining. When the president asked Jackie about the status of the backlog, she referred to a report that showed that her team was three days behind in production. At that point, Aaron spoke up and said, "That's not true. You're closer to eight days behind."

Jackie felt like Aaron "threw her under the bus" in front of her peers, her boss and worst of all, the president. Little did she know that I had heard Aaron's side of the story just a week earlier in my coaching session with him.

According to Aaron, he was tired of hearing the polished version of Jackie's report. In his opinion, the three days that Jackie reported as the number of days her team was behind was not the whole truth. They both knew it would take only three days for Jackie's team to catch up, but only if there was no new business coming in.

In their world, there was no way to halt new business. Aaron believed that saying they were three days behind was giving a false sense of reality to their leadership. Aaron wanted to talk about the reality their department was living. Aaron stated what he saw to be the truth.

Jackie saw Aaron's actions as a lack of loyalty and a breach of trust. Jackie's response? She was giving Aaron the silent treatment. Jackie believed she deserved an apology. The team's cohesiveness had vanished, and their energy was drained as the tension hovered day in and day out.

In my next coaching session with Jackie, she said she didn't trust Aaron anymore. When I asked Jackie about the past five years of collaboration and synergy in working with Aaron, she simply replied, "I guess I've just gotten to know the *real* Aaron in the past month."

Both Jackie and Aaron had valid perspectives. And they had a common goal of seeing the team and the company succeed. The rift between them was rooted in Jackie's perspective that Aaron "threw her under the bus" to get the negative spotlight off himself. When Jackie bought into the belief that Aaron could not be trusted, she began living out her story as if it were true. She looked for confirmation that her assumption was accurate.

So what's at stake for Jackie and Aaron? They think about the tension between them every time they are in the same room. They don't seek each other out to collaborate and brainstorm. The company loses when they don't come up with creative ideas for meeting their goals. The team loses when the synergy and fun is missing from team meetings. They lose the enjoyment and fulfillment they used to have at work. There's much at stake.

It's easy to procrastinate having these challenging conversations. But when we ask ourselves what's at stake, we need to face the reality that the pebbles in our shoes are more than a minor irritation. We're losing productive energy. We're losing our joy.

When we carry pebbles in our shoes, it's distracting. We can't have peace when we're at odds with someone we work with or live with.

Because the thought of tackling these confrontational conversations may leave us with an apprehensive feeling in the pit in our stomach, we need to ask ourselves what's at stake. Unless we come up with a compelling answer, it would be easy to indefinitely procrastinate having these conversations.

Have you ever lost sleep over a conversation that needed to happen? I have. Sleepless nights can turn into health issues if we don't address them. If we let offense creep in, it can escalate into bitterness, which can be toxic not only to our daily mood but also to our long-term health. When we resent another person, somehow we think we're punishing them. But as the saying goes, resenting someone is like drinking rat poison and expecting the rat to die. When we ingest something as toxic as resentment, we are the real victims.

Our relationships are at stake. Our health and happiness are at risk. Where do we begin?

CHAPTER 2

WHAT IS FACT AND WHAT IS STORY?

It was getting late, and my energy was depleted for the day. I walked through the living room, and there was my teenage son sitting on the couch. I thought to myself, "How many times have I asked him to unload the dishes today? It's evening, and that should have been done this morning. Besides that, I'll bet he hasn't done his math assignments yet either. He's becoming so irresponsible and lazy."

"Mitchell," I barked. "How many times have I told you to unload the dishes today? And why are you just sitting on the couch playing a game on your phone when you haven't done your math assignments yet?"

"Mom," Mitchell responded, trying to hold back his annoyance. "Unloading the dishwasher is not my chore this week. And I asked you when you got home from work to help me with my math because I was stuck on the problems I had left. You said you'd help me later."

Oops. Not only was I a terrible listener, but I was also creating quite a story. I had gathered inaccurate evidence and concluded that my son was irresponsible and lazy. My assumptions seemed to justify my anger so I acted on them. My story turned out to be false. Now I owed my son an apology.

I'd like to say that making up stories is a rare occurrence, but it happens more often than I'd like to admit.

What do I mean by "making up stories?" Stories are the assumptions we make that help us interpret a situation. These assumptions are quite convincing and seem both justified and accurate. However, since we really don't know if our assumptions are true, we can't truly claim them as factual. Facts are absolute. No matter how accurate our conclusions feel, they are merely interpretations of the facts. They are stories. And we need to hold them lightly until we can determine if they are true.

Brené Brown, in her book *Rising Strong*, talks about "owning our story." She invites the reader to, "Get honest about the stories we're making up about our struggle, then challenge these confabulations and assumptions to determine what's truth, what's self-protection, and what needs to change if we want to lead more wholehearted lives."[1]

Brown references the work of neurologist Robert Burton when she states that "our brains reward us with dopamine when we recognize and complete patterns. Stories are patterns. The brain recognizes the familiar beginning-middle-end structure of a story and rewards us for clearing up the ambiguity. Unfortunately, we don't need to be accurate, just certain."[2]

Brown goes on to quote Burton, "Because we are compelled to make stories, we are often compelled to take incomplete stories and run with them. Even with half a story in our minds, we earn a dopamine 'reward' every time it helps us understand something in our world—even if that explanation is incomplete or wrong."[3]

Everyone makes up stories. It's natural. But if we are rigid about our perspective and are not willing to entertain the possibility that our stories may be incomplete or faulty, we lack the humility to be curious and open.

Creating stories can lead to accumulating pebbles in our shoes—especially when our energy is depleted or when our mood is negative. Our thinking isn't clear, and when we act on that thinking, we say things we regret and leave casualties in our wake.

Our minds want to make sense of the situation, so we make assumptions. The most dangerous assumption that comes so naturally to us is, "I am right. You are wrong." We then progress to "you are selfish" or "you are intentionally trying to sabotage me." Once we characterize and assign negative intention, we look for ways to reinforce and rationalize our assumptions.

When we don't understand why someone acted as they did, we make up stories. Then we act like these stories are true. That's what gets us into trouble. In order to avoid this tendency and move toward conflict resolution, we need to separate the facts from our stories.

I coach two business partners who own a web design company in Chicago that has experienced significant growth over the past five years. Michele

is laid back and doesn't let much bother her. Joe *Keith*
doesn't care for confrontation, so he goes silent
when something bothers him and then blows up
when he reaches a boiling point.

They had both been struggling with the same
issue. Ironically, each felt they were doing more
than their fair portion of the work, and the other
person wasn't carrying their share of the load. They
didn't talk about it. Instead, they created stories.
Their stories sounded something like this:

> **Michele's story:** I allowed Joe to pull out of the
> day-to-day functions of web design to be the
> operations manager. Now with his extra time
> during the work day, he's playing racquetball
> and doing consulting for extra income on the
> side. He's not being honest with how he's using
> his time, and it's not fair.

> **Joe's story:** We have hired two web designers to
> replace Michele so she can focus on marketing.
> Michele's main priority is to help us grow our
> business. She wants me to help schedule her
> calendar, but when I schedule meetings for her,
> she doesn't show up to the meetings. Then she
> expects me to cover for her at the last minute.

She is irresponsible, and I'm tired of doing everything around here.

Can you see how these stories would affect their day-to-day interactions? They didn't want to discuss these issues with one another because they didn't want to negatively affect the relationship. They thought they were putting up a good façade that everything was fine. But do you think their frustrations were "leaking"? Absolutely.

Up to this point, I had only coached them one-on-one, and that's where I heard each of their stories. I asked them to prepare for a coaching session with the three of us by untangling fact from story. I explained that facts are absolute, and stories are our interpretation of the facts. I encouraged them to take another look at what they believed with this perspective. Then I asked each of them to prepare a list with all the facts in one column and all the stories they had created or perceived to be true in another. Their lists looked like this:

Michele's List

Fact:
- Joe is no longer doing web design.
- Joe is now the operations manager.

- Joe started playing racquetball during the day.
- Joe started offering consulting services to outside clients.

Story:
- Joe is playing racquetball and consulting during the hours he should be working as operations manager.
- Joe's not being honest.
- It's not fair.

Joe's List

Fact:
- We hired two web designers to replace what Michele has been doing on a daily basis.
- Michele's role is to focus on marketing.
- I schedule appointments on Michele's calendar.
- She doesn't show up to meetings I've scheduled for her.

Story:
- Michele expects me to cover for her at the last minute.

- Michele is irresponsible.
- I do everything around here.

When we got together, we started with the facts that each person recorded. They agreed on the facts. Then we started to unpack the stories one at a time. I asked each of them to use the phrase, "The story I'm telling myself is…."[4]

"The story I'm telling myself" is a powerful phrase in two ways. When we admit that it's a story, it helps us hold it lightly. It reminds us that the other person may have a very different story. This phrase helps us be curious and less judgmental. Facts are absolute. Stories are open to interpretation.

The second reason that "The story I'm telling myself…" is so powerful is that it communicates to the other person a sense of openness and humility. When we use that phrase, we are not locked into our opinion as truth, but we are offering our story as our perspective. We are not painting our partner into a corner. We are proposing our story as a hypothesis. If we are willing to change our stories after hearing from the other person's perspective, we are on our way to a learning conversation that breaks down walls.

The step of untangling fact from story is critical in Base Camp, the preparation process. It helps us get curious about how the other person sees the situation.

Now back to Joe and Michele. They were each careful to use the phrase, "The story I'm telling myself is...." The dialogue flowed with very little defensiveness and a significant number of aha moments. They were able to jump into each other's shoes and gain new understanding. By the end of the conversation, they had gathered some significant insights. They had corrected their stories.

Michele learned that Joe was only using an occasional lunch hour to play racquetball. She also learned that he was putting the money he had been earning by consulting back into their business.

Joe learned that Michele was keeping her own calendar, and she wasn't aware that he couldn't view that calendar. When the meetings he scheduled conflicted with the meetings she already had on her calendar, she assumed he wouldn't expect her to attend. They agreed to combine the two calendars so Joe wouldn't double book Michele's appointments. They also agreed to talk each Monday about the upcoming appointments for the week.

While they were hearing each other's perspectives and correcting their stories, they were enriching their relationship. Their trust began to return. They could see each other as well-intentioned individuals who really did want the best for their business and for their working relationship.

CHAPTER 3

WHAT AM I FEELING?

I got a text from one of my coaching clients named Jenn who worked for a credit card company. Jenn asked for a coaching session as soon as possible. When I walked into Jenn's office the next day, she was clearly frustrated. She proceeded to tell me that she was at a dead end with Steve, a peer she worked with daily.

Steve was the manager of a team that was formed to launch a new distribution channel. The top 12 performers on Jenn's team were transitioned to Steve's team to help with the development and launch.

Steve was a hard-working, bright individual who was asked to lead this team because he had been with the company for ten years and his strengths were product knowledge, creativity and tenacity.

Jenn was a collaborative, tenderhearted individual who had been hired from outside the organization three years prior to correct some toxic people issues on a dysfunctional team. She was told she didn't need to know all the intricate functions of the computer system or every procedure done by her team. She was hired to be a generalist and oversee her team.

The day prior to our conversation, Jenn received an email from Steve asking why those who transitioned from Jenn's team didn't know how to do a number of computer processes correctly. From Steve's perspective, this gap in their training was inexcusable, and Jenn was at fault.

Steve and Jenn were going to meet the next day to talk through how they could resolve these training issues and discuss how they could work together more effectively.

I asked Jenn what she was feeling. Jenn said she felt like Steve was demeaning. We talked about the difference between Jenn *feeling* demeaned and Steve *being* demeaning. The impact of Steve's behavior was that Jenn felt demeaned. But for

Jenn to tell Steve that *he* was demeaning was a judgment, not simply a disclosure of Jenn's feelings.

When we talked about how Jenn could address her feelings in the conversation the next day, I recommended she use the phrase, "I know this wasn't your intention, but the impact on me was…."

I gave Jenn an example of how this phrase would work. "I know this wasn't your intention, but when I got an email asking why my team had training gaps, the impact on me was that I felt demeaned."

Jenn told Steve she *felt* demeaned so Steve knew how his behavior impacted her. But Jenn removed judgment and the assumption of ill intent when she said she didn't believe it was Steve's intention to demean her. It protected Steve's dignity and kept any defenses low.

When we own our feelings and don't blame the other person for what we're feeling, we demonstrate we're taking accountability for our own emotions. In addition, we're making the other person aware of their behavior's impact on us. It may seem easier to just avoid talking about feelings because they can be complicated and subjective. But if we skip this step, the other person doesn't fully understand the impact of their behavior. To enrich our relationships and know how to more effectively relate to each other in the future, we need to give the other person this feedback.

Have you ever heard the saying, "When someone spits on you, they don't make you mad. They just make you wet"? Between the action of "getting spit on" and the reaction of "getting mad," we make up a story. Let me illustrate. If a baby spits on you, do you get mad? No. Why not? Because it wasn't the baby's fault. We assign no ill intention, so we don't get upset. It's the story we create between the action and our reaction that elicits either a gracious or an angry response.

There was a historical and biblical figure who got spat on and didn't get mad. Who was that person? Jesus. Why didn't he get mad when he was not only spat on but also beaten and brutally executed? He spoke very little during the beatings and his eventual death. One thing recorded in the Bible that he did say was, "Father, forgive them for they don't know what they're doing."

Jesus forgave the people who were responsible for his death without them even asking for forgiveness. Why? Because he believed they didn't truly understand what they were doing. As a result, Jesus did not get angry. He responded with forgiveness.

When we get angry, it's important to acknowledge our anger. But it's powerful when we also
realize that it's our choice to become angry. To
say, "You **made** me angry" is to place the blame
on someone else for our emotions.

Instead, to say "I **am** angry" is to be accountable
for our emotions. If we recognize that our emotions are a choice, we are empowered to choose a
different emotion. There is power in choice.

When we talk about our feelings, it's important to say "I feel…" instead of "You **made** me
feel…." It helps the other person know we are
taking accountability for how we choose to feel.
The other person is not likely to argue with how
we feel, and even more apt to share their own
feelings as well. It sets a tone of accountability and
openness, which keeps the defenses low.

CHAPTER 4

WHAT COULD HAVE BEEN THEIR INTENTIONS?

We all have lenses we look through to help us make sense of the world, people and situations. It's like wearing a pair of glasses. As we have experiences with people, we gather information about whether we like them, trust them, and if we believe they have good or bad intentions. These experiences become part of the story we tell ourselves and the lens we look through every time we communicate with them.

Imagine your team at work is planning a social event and the team member who got nominated to send out the invitations is your most difficult person at work. You "walk on eggshells" around her and you feel tension with her most days. Your other co-workers begin receiving their invitations to the social event. You never receive an invitation. What is the story you tell yourself? She intentionally left you off the list, right?

Let's change the situation with only one detail. Let's say the co-worker who sent out the invitations is your best friend at work instead of your most difficult co-worker. Same outcome—you don't receive an invitation. What's the story you tell yourself this time? She didn't mean to leave you off the list. You're sure it was an accident. Or maybe she didn't think you needed an invitation because you already knew all the details from your conversations at breaks.

The action was the same. The story you told yourself about intention was absolutely opposite. The root of almost every conflict is the assumption that the other person has negative intentions. We create stories. And then we act as if they're true. Our natural tendency is to look for reinforcement of our stories.

To properly prepare for a conflict resolution conversation, we need to get off "autopilot" and ask ourselves two unnatural questions, "How could a reasonable person do what they did? How could their behavior have made sense to them?"

Instead of buying into the story that they had bad intentions, can we, for a moment, assume they had good intentions? People do what makes sense to them. If their intentions were, in fact, good, what might those intentions be? Can we get curious enough to ponder this question?

Ultimately, we can't know their intentions unless they tell us. But we will be in a better place emotionally and clearer in our thinking if we go through the exercise of asking ourselves what it would be like to be in their skin. Once we intentionally get curious as a part of our preparation for the conversation, we are better able to communicate with genuine curiosity in the face-to-face conversation. When we move from judgment to curiosity, the other person will sense our desire to understand rather than blame.[1]

I was the Director of Training at a company early in my career. A part of my role was to process tuition reimbursement requests for employees who chose to further their education. One day I got a reimbursement form requesting three times the maximum amount allowed for any employee. I saw the name of the manager this employee reported to, Melanie, and noticed she was part of a team that was a startup division at a new location. This team of managers had a reputation at the home office for getting whatever they requested because the startup division was so phenomenally successful. When I saw the request, it immediately reinforced my perception that this team thought they could ask for the moon and have it delivered on a silver platter.

As I mumbled under my breath, I left my office and began sharing my story with my other human resource colleagues. They kindly listened and empathized. I left the conversation feeling justified in my judgment.

I made my way back to my office and decided I had better confront the situation. I picked up the phone to place a call to Melanie. In that moment, I made a split decision to ask a question first and refrain from sharing my judgmental perspective upfront. When Melanie answered the phone, I greeted her and then mustered up a curious question, "Can you give me the background on this tuition reimbursement request from your new team member?"

"Oh, I'm sorry," Melanie responded immediately. "I should have called you. Let me explain what happened. We needed to fill a key role in our division and we found the perfect person at a competing company. She was willing to come to work for us on one condition—that we would match the educational benefits she was receiving from her former employer until she graduated." Melanie said she had received permission from every member of her upline, but apologized for not informing me before she sent the form.

There I sat holding my empty story. I instantly felt guilty for creating a villainous picture of Melanie. And I really wished I had kept my negative story to myself instead of sharing the poison with my colleagues. I had a sinking feeling because I knew the right thing to do. I needed to rectify the story. I felt embarrassed as I told my co-workers the real reason behind the request for tuition reimbursement. Had I held my story lightly and withheld my judgment, I would have not only saved face but also avoided tarnishing the mood of my team.

When other people's behaviors don't make sense to us, it's natural to make assumptions. Are these assumptions usually positive or negative? In the heat of the moment, it's more natural to assume negative intentions.

Once we make negative assumptions about another person, it affects the lens we look through when we interpret that person's every action. It's natural to look for reinforcement for the story we are telling ourselves. We latch onto everything that confirms the story we have already made up.

If we pause and ask ourselves the question, "What am I assuming right now?" we can get in tune with our stories. A clue as to whether we are making positive or negative assumptions is our mood. Are we irritated, frustrated or annoyed? If so, we are most likely making up negative stories.[2] The good news is that we can decide to consider more positive stories. How? By simply asking, "How would a reasonable person do what they did?"

People do what makes sense to them. With their current level of thinking, they choose what seems to be their best option. We may think they have made a poor choice. If so, it would be easy to resort to a judgmental response. But between their action and our reaction, we have a choice to make. We can either get judgmental, or we can get curious. When we get judgmental, irritated or frustrated, who pays the biggest price? We do. If we can choose to be curious, inquisitive and respectful, who benefits most? We do. If we can stay open minded long enough to wonder how that person's behavior made sense to them, we can maintain clearer thinking and a more positive mood.

CHAPTER 5

WHAT PART HAVE I PLAYED?

My husband, Troy, is a real estate agent. Some friends of ours from our neighborhood, Jeff and Karen, were selling their home because Jeff's career was taking him out of state. After two weeks on the market, Jeff and Karen were getting anxious. Their time frame was short, and they needed to sell quickly in order for Jeff to start his new job on time.

Troy decided to host a "Realtor open house" to expose the home to more agents and to solicit professional feedback for the sellers. After the open house, the predominant feedback from the agents was that the house was priced well but needed some new carpet and a few rooms needed to be painted in more neutral colors. When Troy passed this information along to Jeff and Karen, Karen burst into tears. She felt insulted that the agents didn't like her taste in colors. The next day, Jeff sent Troy an email and said they felt insulted and wanted to pull their listing immediately. They would sell it themselves.

Troy wrote a lengthy email in response, apologizing to both of them for Karen's embarrassment and said he wished the best for them in the sale of their home and the start of their new life. Jeff and Karen did not respond.

It consumed Troy's energy for a number of days. It affected my energy and mood too. We were organizing a block party the following weekend, and we were confident they would be there. Our natural response was to avoid them. And that's what we did. We acted like they weren't there, but in reality, they consumed our attention.

A month later, the neighbors gathered for a picnic to wish Jeff and Karen farewell. Troy was showing houses to some clients so he was unable to attend. As I mentally prepared myself to see Jeff and Karen at the picnic, I reflected on how much I believed in the power of conversation. I knew conflicts could be resolved and rifts could be mended if we started by admitting the part we had played in the conflict. I was nervous but knew I needed to find an opportunity to have a conversation with Karen.

I talked to a number of people at the picnic and then saw out of the corner of my eye that Karen was available. I approached her and started by saying that Troy and I hoped they had successfully closed on their home. Karen confirmed that they had. I told her that Troy was horribly sorry about how humiliated she felt after their last conversation. I asked her if she had received Troy's email apologizing. She confirmed that she had.

Karen explained that she was under extreme stress at the time Troy gave her the feedback about their home needing some repainting. All the pressure she had been suppressing from multiple sources came to a head, and it was at that moment she fell apart. She apologized for not responding to Troy's email.

I admitted that we had let the tension fester and that we had been avoiding them. I apologized for cutting off the communication. She gave me a hug and said, "Thank you for being so gracious."

The tension was resolved. The relationship was restored.

I have coached countless people on how to resolve their conflicts, but when it was my own conflict I needed to address, I must confess I wanted to procrastinate. I had to remind myself that the silent treatment is toxic to a relationship. When we shut out the other person, the relationship shrinks. We can't solve problems in silence.[1]

When we are willing to make the first move and break the silence, the other person is likely to turn toward us in response. When we admit we have contributed to the problem, it removes the blame and creates an environment of humility. We extend our hand, and the other person will likely extend their hand in return. As we admit our contribution to the issue, there's a good chance the other person will take accountability for some part as well.

Sometimes it's difficult to identify what part we've played in a conflict situation. What we did makes sense to us, and we've justified it. But if we can get reflective and consider all the factors that contributed to a conflict, it's usually not entirely the other person's fault.

If we can claim some responsibility for the very results with which we are unhappy, then this has two critical benefits. First, when we resist the urge to put all the blame on the other person, we are more apt to see them as a partner rather than an opponent.[2] The tone of the conversation will undoubtedly be more open and receptive. Secondly, when we identify our contribution to the issue, we become aware of choices we made that led to the conflict. It reminds us that if we make different choices going forward, we can get different results. Choices are empowering, and we often have more choices than we realize.

CHAPTER 6

WHAT CURIOUS QUESTIONS CAN I ASK TO CREATE SAFETY?

The final step in the Base Camp process is to select questions that set a tone of safety and openness. When we shift from judgment to curiosity in our thinking, it's critical we ask questions that reflect this open mindset.

Going into the conversation with a desire to learn (rather than to prove we are right, and the other person is wrong) will lead to a conversation that enriches the relationship. These types of conversations are also at the core of personal growth and new insight.

I often ask people attending my coaching work-shops to consider who has been an official or unofficial coach for them. People tell stories of a sports coach who believed in their potential. Or a sister with whom they could share everything without feeling judged. Or a friend who could give them constructive feedback without offending them. Then I ask the follow-up question, "What is the quality of those relationships that allows you to take their honest feedback without getting offended?" The consistent answer is, "I know that person has my best interest in mind."

When we sincerely want the best for another person, they will sense our authenticity by the questions we ask.

One of the best ways to keep defenses low in a conflict resolution conversation is to choose questions that communicate curiosity rather than judgment. To do this, it's helpful to avoid asking "why" questions. Even though a why question may seem curious in our minds, there is a subtle assumption of blame in a why question. Let me illustrate.

What is the difference between the question, "Why were you late?" and "What prevented you from being on time?" Do you sense the subtle tone of blame in the why question and the assumption of innocence in the what question? The second question protects the other person's dignity and gives him the benefit of the doubt. It communicates curiosity rather than judgment.

Amy set up an appointment with me to talk about a challenge she was having with her manager, Deb. When she arrived, she told me that Deb was headstrong and demanding. Amy shared that in the last team meeting, Deb presented an idea that Amy disagreed with. Deb had been encouraging Amy to speak up in meetings more often, so she thought this would be a good opportunity to give it a try. Amy started by saying, "Deb, I think you're wrong." Amy continued with, "Why do we have to do that procedure a new way? It's a lot more complicated than you think and the old way works just fine." Deb got defensive. The team meeting got tense. Amy said she was not sure she would ever speak up in a team meeting again.

I explained that when someone gets defensive, it's helpful to ask ourselves if there was something we said to trigger that defensive response. Amy struggled to identify a trigger she could take accountability for. I suggested that the statement "you're wrong" normally elicits a defensive reaction.

In addition, why questions move people to a position of having to defend themselves. When people feel backed into a corner, they are no longer receptive to a new perspective. Their energy shifts to defending themselves. The atmosphere of openness and learning disintegrates into defensiveness and self-protection.

One of the best ways to avoid this scenario is to communicate a genuine interest in understanding the other person's perspective. To see someone else's point of view, you need to temporarily suspend your perspective just long enough to jump into her shoes and gain an understanding of her viewpoint. Once you understand her perspective, you can decide if you want to toggle back to your own opinion. But in the process of being willing to see another's point of view, you gain another perspective to consider. Because you've been open to the other person's point of view, she feels valued and understood. You create emotional safety.

Emotional safety is the state in which "each individual is open and vulnerable.... When a relationship is emotionally safe, the partners trust each other and routinely give each other the benefit of the doubt in questionable situations. When emotional safety is lost, the partners are inclined to be distrustful, looking for possible hidden meanings and potential threats in each other's words and behaviors."[1]

I got a text from a young woman named Leah whom I had worked with at a non-profit organization. She said she needed to talk and wondered if I would meet with her. The next day we went out for coffee, and she began to share her story. Leah had just announced to family and friends that she was engaged to Jeremy. Leah's family didn't know Jeremy very well because they had only been dating about six months and Leah and Jeremy lived in a city quite distant from Leah's family.

As the congratulations began to circulate, Leah's brother Andy heard through the grapevine that Jeremy had a history of drug use and had gone to prison for dealing drugs five years earlier. Andy called Leah and asked her if she was aware of Jeremy's past. Leah was not.

When Leah asked Jeremy about it, he confessed that what Andy told her was true. He also admitted that he was afraid to tell Leah this part of his past because he was afraid she would leave him. After many late nights, tears and intense conversations, Leah forgave Jeremy for not disclosing this part of his past sooner. And Jeremy reassured her of his commitment to being fully transparent from that point on and completely free of drugs in the future.

Jeremy and Leah's relationship matured from this conflict they had resolved. In the meantime, Leah's brother Andy grew increasingly suspicious about what other secrets Jeremy may be keeping. Since Andy lived a significant distance away, the opportunity to connect face to face with Jeremy was rare. Attempts by both Jeremy and Andy to communicate through email failed to facilitate any level of reconciliation. Jeremy became discouraged. Andy decided he would not attend the wedding. He explained to the other members of the family why he didn't trust Jeremy and why he felt Leah was making a mistake in marrying Jeremy.

Leah's mother, Julie, was also devastated when she heard the news about Jeremy's past and that he had hidden it from Leah until he was confronted. Julie knew that even though Jeremy and Leah may have worked through this issue between them, the trust still needed to be restored with the rest of the family. They needed confirmation that Leah wasn't being deceived about who Jeremy truly was.

Julie wrestled with how she could ever restore her trust in Jeremy. She spent much time in tears and on her knees in prayer. She felt like God was asking her to soften her heart toward Jeremy and to be open to the possibility that he had changed.

Julie determined she would start by getting together with Jeremy to ask curious questions about his background, to ask how he was processing the tension with the family, and to determine how she could support him in his relationship with Leah. She wanted to understand his heart. She wanted Jeremy to be real with her. She didn't intend to "let him off the hook" for what he had done, but she knew she needed to soften her heart and begin to understand his story in order for him to open up to her.

Julie started the conversation with Jeremy by letting him know that she wanted a good relationship with him, and that she wanted what was best for him and Leah. Julie found common ground with Jeremy, and she made it safe. She turned her heart toward Jeremy, and she began to see him through a new lens.

As Jeremy sensed Julie's acceptance, he began to share his story. His authenticity began to emerge because Julie had made it safe for him to be open. She asked curious questions about his journey, his struggles, his pain. She began to realize that he was a young man who was afraid—and truly sorry for both his drug use and the hiding of his past. She learned that Jeremy was on a journey toward honesty and transparency. This conversation between Julie and Jeremy was a new start. Julie began to develop a motherly love for Jeremy.

Leah's brother Andy, on the other hand, chose to stay "locked into" his opinion of Jeremy. He declined the opportunity to get to know Jeremy and chose to stand on his story that Jeremy still could not be trusted. This decision caused tension at family holidays and built walls among the members of a once close-knit family.

Both curiosity and judgment are a choice. It requires humility to ask curious questions and be open to learning a new perspective. It calls us to do what's seemingly unnatural and certainly more difficult.

When we think we're right, it's natural to "lock into" that opinion and feel a sense of self-righteousness. But this certainty and rigidity not only "locks out" the other person's story, but it also locks out a transparent, open relationship.[2]

Curiosity, on the other hand, is the key that unlocks their story. It gives us the option to learn from their perspective. Here's the reality—just because I hear another person's story with openness doesn't mean I have to abandon my perspective and embrace his. I can listen to his story and decide afterward if I want to change my mind. Even if I choose to disagree, I can live with open dialogue and differing opinions easier than rigidity and close-minded thinking.

Determining curious questions to ask is more of a mindset than it is a task. If we are willing to set aside all judgment and ask, "How did his behavior make sense to her?" and, "What's it like to walk in her shoes?" we will be prepared for a productive conflict resolution conversation.

If we want another person to open up to us, we need to create a safe place for him to be real. No one wants to make himself vulnerable with a person who is judgmental, blaming and critical. The key to unlocking safety and, ultimately, an authentic relationship, is offering another person respect and unconditional positive regard. When we extend acceptance without conditions, we make it safe for the other person to share his perspective and give him the desire to listen to our point of view in return. We set a tone of openness and learning that leads to a productive conversation.

CHAPTER 7

HOW WILL I START
THE CONVERSATION?

You have completed preparations in Base Camp by reflecting on the following questions:

- What's at stake?
- What is fact and what is story?
- What am I feeling?
- What could have been their intentions?
- What part have I played?
- What curious questions can I ask to create safety?

When you take the time to prepare each of the preceding elements of Base Camp, your heart and mind will be in a good place before the conversation even begins. To ensure that the dialogue begins with both safety and clarity, prepare an opening statement. This statement should take no longer than a minute to present. If it takes longer than a minute, it may sound like a lecture and the other person may tune you out.[1]

You will want to write out your opening statement initially, but be familiar enough with it that you don't need to read it during the actual conversation. The statement will include many of your thoughts and reflections from Base Camp. The elements of the statement are the steps we will explore in our next section—the Ascent:

- State the issue without blame
- Give one or two examples
- Share what part I've played
- Invite them to give their perspective

It's time to invite the other person into the conversation.

STEP 2

ASCENT: THE CONVERSATION

Before we begin our Ascent, I want to address what happens if the other person declines your invitation to talk. This has happened to me.

Stacy and I were board members for a nonprofit organization that we were both passionate about. It seemed very clear to me that Stacy didn't like me. When I asked her a question, she answered with one word. If I gave her a compliment, she gave me no response at all. I knew that I must have had a part in creating this strained relationship, but I didn't know what I had done.

I decided to write her a letter to share my impressions and invite her to talk. In the letter, I expressed concern over the tension in our relationship and that I believed it affected our ability to work together cohesively on the board. I apologized for whatever part I played. I asked her if she would be willing to have a conversation in order to give me insights on what I could do to make our relationship better. I mailed the letter with hope and anticipation.

About a week later, I received a response from Stacy in the mail. She thanked me for my letter, but she said she was not ready to talk about the issues between us.

Now what?

I was still left to wonder. The tension was not going to vanish on its own. What were my choices?

After much thinking, praying and reflecting, I came to a place where I knew that what Stacy was doing made sense to her, even though it didn't make sense to me. If Stacy had shared with me the reason she kept her distance, I would have understood her story and her rationale. But since I was not going to get that awareness at this point or perhaps ever, I had two choices. I could build the wall higher between us and blame Stacy for it, or I could give her the freedom to be herself and choose to show her love and acceptance.

I could not control Stacy's actions, but I could certainly choose my own attitude and behavior in response to her. Despite the temptation to play the role of a victim and become resentful, it was my responsibility to keep my heart soft toward Stacy, regardless of her decision to keep her thoughts private.

Up to the time of this writing, I still have not had the opportunity to resolve this conflict with Stacy even though our paths still cross on occasion. Does it hurt? Absolutely. It's a wound that's been in my spirit for many years. It's been a personal battle for me, but I respect Stacy's choice to keep her thoughts to herself. If she ever gets to the point that she feels she can have that conversation with me, I want her to feel like the invitation is still open.

So what happens if we invite the other person to talk and they accept our invitation? Then it's time to act on the preparation we've done in Base Camp. It's time to climb the mountain. It's time to begin our Ascent.

CHAPTER 8

STATE THE ISSUE WITHOUT BLAME

I walked into the retail store owned by one of my coaching clients, Antonio. Once we settled into his office, I asked him what he'd like to discuss in our coaching session that day.

Antonio sighed and said, "The timing of this coaching session is impeccable. We have a new member of our team who is driving everyone crazy. I'm hoping you can help me come up with some better strategies than I've come up with on my own."

Antonio proceeded to share with me that Dominic had joined the sales team two months ago. He came with a great track record and was a top performer on the sales team where he had previously worked. With his past success, Dominic seemed to think his best practices should be immediately implemented on Antonio's sales team. Dominic frequently corrected the seasoned sales representatives according to how he thought they should be approaching their customers. He also privately complained to one co-worker about another.

Frustrated team members often confided in Antonio and soon many hours of his week were consumed with his sales representatives' stories about Dominic's negative behavior. Antonio knew he needed to confront Dominic, but he didn't know where to begin.

We talked about the elements of Base Camp and how to prepare for the conversation. Antonio recognized that he needed to start by stating the issue without blaming Dominic in order to keep the defenses low. We discussed the pattern of behavior that was getting in Dominic's way. He was offending people in his efforts to give them feedback. He was also using triangular communication—going to a third party instead of directly to the source—to vent about other team members.

In order to state the issue without blame and get the conversation started with a non-defensive but clear direction, Antonio decided to begin the conversation as follows, "Dominic, I would like to talk with you about how your communication style is impacting the team." This approach stated Dominic's pattern of behavior clearly. But it was free of blame, so it didn't trigger defensiveness in Dominic. Antonio and Dominic had a successful start to their Ascent.

Let's talk about what happens when a conversation gets defensive. Once people get triggered, their energy shifts from learning and openness to defending themselves and protecting their dignity. There is a scientific explanation for why this happens. In the book *Crucial Conversations*, authors Patterson, Grenny, McMillan and Switzler explain that when we feel a real or perceived threat, the fight-or-flight response is triggered. The blood flowing to the higher functioning parts of our brain—the parts that helps us respond intelligently—gets hijacked. The blood flow is redirected to our large muscle groups in preparation for fight or flight.[1]

This explains why when we get defensive, we are more prepared to punch someone than we are to say something intelligent. Just when we need our brain the most, it deserts us. That's why we can leave casualties in our wake and have to do damage control later. It's to our advantage to keep the defenses low and keep both parties operating with their highest caliber of thinking.

Another way to communicate openness rather than blame is to avoid particular words that trigger a defensive response. Saying "we" instead of "you" as much as possible communicates that the two of you are in this together. The conversation is about exploration, not combat.[2] Secondly, as we've already established, it's best to avoid why questions. "Why" has an overtone of judgment, putting people in the psychological position of having to defend themselves.

Trudy, the president of a company I work with, was frustrated with the communication style of one of her direct reports, Keith. Trudy was a bottom-line focused person and Keith was extremely social. From Trudy's perspective, Keith used three times more words than necessary in any conversation. She wanted him to get to the point.

In coaching sessions with Keith, I learned that he was frustrated in his conversations with Trudy as well. From his perspective, when he presented a new idea to Trudy, she didn't give him the immediate feedback he was looking for so he assumed she needed more information. He kept talking, thinking that would help elicit a response from her.

Shortly after I heard both leaders express frustration with each other's communication style, I had the opportunity to facilitate a team-building session with them and their team. In that session, I included a feedback exercise in which I gave them each the opportunity to share how they could better communicate with one another. In that exercise, Trudy gave Keith the feedback that she would prefer him to use two or three sentences to share a new idea or opinion and then stop talking. Keith looked surprised. He paused and then sincerely thanked Trudy for her feedback.

In my next coaching session with Keith, he said this communication exercise was a breakthrough for him. He realized that using more words to engage Trudy was actually having the opposite effect of what he wanted. Since the team building session, he had begun to state his points in two or three sentences. With a smile on his face, he said he had already seen better results in his communication with Trudy.

Trudy gave Keith the gift of feedback. What Keith became aware of, he had the choice to change.

Before Keith was aware of Trudy's preference for succinct communication, it was a blind spot for him. He now knew to condense his communication to get better results in his working relationship with Trudy. She presented the feedback to Keith clearly and without blaming him. She stated her preferences. With his new awareness, Keith could flex his communication style to be more effective in presenting his opinions and new ideas to Trudy. That was a win-win conversation.

CHAPTER 9

GIVE ONE OR TWO EXAMPLES

Ted was the president of an online business. He told me in a recent coaching session that he was getting ready to promote a young woman named Emily. When Ted told Emily this good news and outlined her new responsibilities, Emily asked Ted who would be training her. Ted informed Emily that Laura would be her trainer. Emily said she was excited about the opportunity, but she was hesitant to work with Laura. When Ted asked Emily to elaborate, she said she didn't trust Laura because she had been sabotaging Emily's success for about six months. Emily went on to give a couple of examples to support her belief.

Ted knew that Emily and Laura needed to partner not only for the training period but also going forward in Emily's new position. Collaboration and trust between them were critical for Emily to be successful in her new role.

Ted and I laid out a plan for him to facilitate a conversation between Emily and Laura in order to resolve the trust issues between them. A critical part of this conversation was for Emily to give one or two examples of Laura's behavior that led Emily to create the story that Laura was sabotaging Emily's success.

If Emily was not able to provide any examples for Laura, she would have no idea what she needed to explain or change. Emily owed it to Laura to give her at least one example to help her realize the impact of her behavior on Emily. This new awareness would then give Laura the opportunity to share her perspective and help restore the trust between them.

It was important for Emily to focus on one or two examples at the most. If Emily were to give three, four or five examples, Laura would likely feel like it was a dumping session and could easily get defensive and shut down in the process.

As Emily prepared her examples, it was critical that she remain objective and remove judgment and blame. I recommended that Ted coach Emily to share her examples with Laura objectively—as if a video camera was recording them. It was important to talk about facts rather than opinions. Laura would be more receptive to objective details than assumptions.

The first example Emily prepared to share with Laura was an incident when Ted had asked Emily to write a new telephone script to help one of her team members, Matt, be more effective in making sales calls. Emily created the script and passed it on to Matt. When Matt began using the script in his phone calls, it felt cumbersome and awkward. Before he said anything to Emily, he told Laura about his challenges using the script. Laura decided to develop her own script for Matt to try. She gave it to Matt without making either Emily or Ted aware. Matt found he preferred Laura's script over Emily's, so rather than working with Emily to revise her script, Matt discarded Emily's script and began using Laura's script exclusively. When Emily heard that Laura had created a new script for Matt, Emily said she felt undermined.

The second example occurred when Emily was talking casually with Matt one day. Matt told Emily that he and Laura had been discussing the new computer program that Emily had just released to the team for calculating sales bonuses. Matt told Emily that Laura thought it would be a good test for Emily's program to enter in some faulty data to see if her new program was effective enough to catch it. Emily was offended and felt like this was evidence that Laura was actively working against Emily.

As Emily prepared to have this conversation with Laura, Ted coached her to be objective in her examples. In order to demonstrate that Emily was doing her best to assume positive intentions on Laura's part, Ted recommended she use the statement, "I know this wasn't your intention, but the impact on me was that I felt undermined." With this statement, Emily would avoid assigning ill intentions to Laura's actions, but still make her aware of how her actions impacted Emily.

Citing examples objectively, like a video camera would record them, keeps the defenses low and the conversation flowing.

CHAPTER 10

SHARE WHAT PART I'VE PLAYED

Once we've stated the issue without blaming the other person and given one or two examples from an objective perspective, it's important to share our contribution to the issue. What part have we played in the very situation that has caused us frustration or disappointment? If we claim some accountability, it will keep the defenses low and communicate that we are partnering with the other person to solve the problem, not fighting against the other person to win a battle. The preparation we've done in Base Camp will help us articulate this part of the Ascent conversation.

Melanie walked into my office and asked if I had a moment to talk. I invited her to take a seat.

When I asked her what was on her mind, she said she had received an email from Kristen (one of her team members) earlier that day, and she was still trying to digest it. In the email, Kristen said she had noticed there was a great deal of tension between them lately. She didn't know what the problem was, but felt as if Melanie was giving off an aloof vibe.

After Melanie worked through a natural tendency to be defensive, she admitted that reading people's emotions and sensing the tone of a conversation were not her strength. We talked about how she could approach Kristen and determine ways to improve their relationship. As Melanie thought through how she could start the conversation with Kristen, we discussed what Melanie could claim as her part in the tension between them. She decided she would let Kristen know that she wasn't naturally gifted at sensing the tone in the room or being aware of the vibe she was projecting. She would ask Kristen to help coach her on what she could do differently to be more approachable.

When we share our contribution in a conflict resolution conversation, it reinforces that we are in partnership with the other person, not in opposition. Sharing in the accountability also keeps the defenses low and the conversation productive. It communicates humility and lets the other person know that we are not pinning this issue all on them. We are owning the situation and willing to do our part to come to a resolution. The other person will sense that "we are in this together" and we are combining our efforts to enrich the relationship.

CHAPTER 11

INVITE THEM TO GIVE THEIR PERSPECTIVE

Our preparation in Base Camp helps us with the Ascent conversation up until this point. We have stated the issue without blame, given one or two examples and then shared our contribution to the issue. We are now ready to invite them to give their perspective. This is where the bulk of the conversation takes place. We cannot script this portion or fully anticipate how this part of the conversation will unfold. But the preparation in Base Camp is critical for both this uncharted territory and our opening statement as well.

When we have shifted from judgment to curiosity, making the transition from assuming negative intention to assuming positive intention, we are ready to have a conversation filled with learning and insights. When we are ready to own our part in the conflict and willing to jump into their shoes to understand their perspective, the other person will sense our humility and sincerity. We will set a tone of openness that will likely be reciprocated.

When I am out of town on business travel, I usually call each evening to check in with my family. On one occasion, my husband, Troy, answered his cell phone and proceeded to tell me about a confrontation that occurred in our cul-de-sac that afternoon between our son Ian and the neighbor boy Ryan. Ian, who was five at the time, had hit Ryan on the arm with a shovel. Ryan's father, Eric, rushed outside when he heard Ryan burst into tears. Eric reprimanded Ian and then crossed the cul-de-sac to knock on our door and tell Troy what had happened.

As Troy and I were talking that evening, I anticipated what was coming next. As predicted, Troy gave his best sales pitch as to why this matter should be addressed by the parent who resolves conflicts for a living, rather than the parent who was on the scene following the shovel incident.

When I arrived home the next day, I decided to gather some additional data of my own. I first asked our son Ian what had happened from his perspective. He informed me that when he and Ryan were playing, Ian had told Ryan to back up because Ian was getting ready to swing the shovel. Ryan didn't budge, but Ian swung the shovel anyway. From Ian's perspective, he had given Ryan fair warning, so it wasn't his fault Ryan got hurt. Ian didn't see why he needed to apologize.

I knew that whether or not Ian was willing to apologize, I needed to apologize for my son's behavior. I decided I didn't want to march over to the neighbor's home and awkwardly ring the doorbell. I thought I would make it seem more natural. So each evening when I got home from work, I stalked my neighbors from my front window, waiting for the perfect opportunity. On day three, I saw Ryan and Eric on their front lawn doing some yard work. I looked at Ian and said, "We're going over to Ryan's house. Are you ready to apologize?"

"Maybe," responded Ian.

Thinking that maybe this was as good as I was going to get from him, I said to myself, "I'm going with a maybe."

I grabbed Ian's hand, and we made our way across the cul-de-sac.

When we arrived on their front lawn, I began the conversation with, "It takes a cul-de-sac to raise my son. I'm sorry for what happened between the boys earlier this week. Ian, do you have something you'd like to say?"

"I'm sorry," Ian said quietly, but sincerely.

Eric's face softened and said, "It's OK, buddy. Just be more careful next time, OK?"

Ian nodded and quickly scampered off to play with Ryan.

I lingered for a few minutes to talk. I asked Eric about his perspective on the incident. I asked curious questions to understand what he saw as the problem and the solution. He said he noticed the boys had a tendency to get into mischief when they were together if they weren't supervised. He thought it would be good to keep a better eye on them when they played. We both agreed to be more attentive when they were together.

As I walked back home, I sensed that peace had returned to the cul-de-sac. Eric and I had talked, found common ground and heard each other's point of view. I felt lighter in my step as I walked through the doorway of my home.

With the hard work of the Ascent behind us, we can now enjoy the view. The Summit awaits us.

STEP 3

SUMMIT: THE GRATIFICATION

CHAPTER 12

COME TO AN AGREEMENT

Shelly stopped me in the hallway after a meeting and asked if I had a minute to talk. We stepped into a vacant conference room, and she began to tell her story. Shelly had only one other person on her team, Luke, and he was driving her crazy. Shelly said Luke was coming in late, taking 90-minute lunch breaks and taking personal phone calls during the day. She had gotten to the point that she was seething at her desk and didn't even want to look at him when he talked to her. Shelly said she had talked with their manager, Danielle, a number of times, but she didn't think Danielle had addressed the issue because Luke's behavior hadn't changed at all.

I asked Shelly what she was willing to do in order to resolve the tension. She ruled out having the conversation one-on-one with Luke because she thought she would simply lose her temper and be in a worse predicament. She said she preferred to have me present to help facilitate a conversation. I sensed I needed to get her manager's perspective on the situation, so I asked Shelly for permission to talk with Danielle.

When I met with Danielle, she said she was aware of Shelly's complaints but didn't see a need to confront Luke because even with Luke's late arrivals and long lunches, he was getting just as much work done as Shelly was. Since they were both salaried employees, Danielle had a "just get your work done" philosophy. In our conversation, she realized more fully that Luke's behavior was perceived as a lack of accountability by Shelly and was creating a demotivating working environment for her. Danielle agreed that maybe it was time to address Luke's behavior.

I asked Danielle for permission to meet with Luke and get his perspective. In my conversation with Luke, my intention was to hear his story, not share Shelly's story. It was up to Shelly to share her story with Luke. I simply asked Luke about his working relationship with Shelly. Luke knew that something was bothering her, but he had no idea what it was. She seemed moody and dismissive. He wasn't sure from day to day whether she'd be happy or disgruntled. I asked if he'd be willing to talk with her about how to make their working relationship better. He agreed to have the conversation, but only if there was someone to facilitate the dialogue.

I asked both Shelly and Luke to do some homework in advance of our conflict resolution conversation. I asked each of them to complete the following statements about the other person, adapted from the writing of Dennis and Michelle Reina in their book, *Trust and Betrayal in the Workplace:*[1]

1. What I appreciate about you is…
2. What works in our relationship is…
3 What could work better in our relationship is…
4. What I need from you is…
5. Let's brainstorm together ways in which we can work together even better.

I asked Shelly and Luke to bring their prepared answers to the conversation, and this became the outline to guide our discussion. The first two statements would set the tone for a positive conversation. These affirming comments were the only "deposits" these two had made in each other's emotional bank account for months. The interactions leading up to this meeting had been strained, and there had been only "withdrawals" made from each other's emotional bank account. They were overdrawn with each other, and the rapport was at an all-time low. The preparation of these positive statements helped Luke and Shelly remember that they did see value in each other. It helped set a collaborative tone for the conversation.

They had three days to complete their homework. Then Luke, Shelly and their manager, Danielle, came to my office. I asked Shelly and Luke to begin with statements of appreciation for the expertise they each brought to their team. They recalled incidents when they worked together effectively to face a number of production crises head on. It was a good reminder of what worked in their relationship.

When we transitioned to what could work better in their relationship, they were in for some aha moments.

Shelly shared with Luke that his late arrivals and long lunches were a strain on her day because she had to cover for him. Luke, in turn, shared that he was newly divorced and was adjusting to being a single dad. His late arrivals were related to getting his kids to school. His long lunch hours and personal phone calls were used to talk with teachers about some behavioral problems his son was having after his divorce.

Luke learned that his long lunch hours and frequent personal phone calls felt like a lack of accountability to Shelly. He realized that his lack of openness about his life outside of work led Shelly to create stories that Luke was disrespectful and that he assumed Shelly would cover for him without explanation.

They committed to having better communication and clearer expectations. From their discussion, I asked them to form a team agreement. It looked like this:

Team Agreement

1. We will use our online team calendar to record appointments and anticipated late arrivals.

2. If one of us has an unanticipated delay and isn't able to arrive by 8:00 a.m., that person agrees to email or call the other person to ensure they can provide coverage.

3. We will inform each other if we have meetings over our lunch breaks that may exceed 60 minutes.

After they had formed their team agreement, I explained that there would likely be violations of the agreement. Prior to their agreement, there were no violations, only assumptions about how the other person should behave.[2] The agreement brought clarity and expectations to their working relationship. So how would they address violations? They agreed to discuss violations at their weekly team meetings. In addition, the four of us agreed to meet in a month for a check-in. Stay tuned for the rest of the story.

Making an agreement is a critical step at the close of a conflict resolution conversation. If we have sincerely gotten curious and jumped into the other person's shoes, we will have gained a new perspective. We will have grown in our awareness. Next, we need to move from awareness to action. We need to act differently if we want our relationships to be different.

CHAPTER 13

COMMIT TO ACTION

It might seem awkward to change habits of behavior and treat each other differently after working through a conflict. But the truth is, once we gain new insight, our thinking changes. Our attitude also changes when our perspective changes. So our new behaviors will be a natural result of our new thinking. We don't need to pretend like there's no conflict. We have resolved the conflict, and our actions are a reflection of our new thinking and attitude toward the other person.

When we are no longer suppressing our true feelings, our behaviors are naturally aligned with our thinking. This brings with it a sense of integrity and inner peace.

Even though our behaviors will be a natural outflow of our new thinking, admittedly, there may be times when we fall back into old patterns of behavior.

When my son Ian was four, he sat chattering on my lap one day while I was trying to respond to an email.

"Mom," he said.

I was deep in thought and didn't even notice he had said my name.

"Mom…Mom," he said again persistently.

I gave him no response, still focused on formulating my email response to a client. Attempting a different strategy, he reached up and put one small hand on each side of my face. He pulled my head down so my eyes met his.

"Listen to me with your eyes," he said intently.

Busted! He finally got my attention.

That was an aha moment for me. I was slighting one of the most important people in my life. I needed to practice being more fully present. I needed to be more in tune.

Even though I had this insight a number of years ago, I must confess that I need to consistently recommit to the intention of being fully present with my family.

Just the other day, Ian, who is now eight, asked me when we were going to go out on a date. He said it had been too long since we had gone out for ice cream and told each other jokes—his idea of quality time. He was craving my undivided attention, and I needed to renew the commitment I had made when he was a four-year-old sitting on my lap at the computer.

CHAPTER 14

CHECK IN FOR A TUNE-UP

Danielle, Shelly and Luke were back in my office for their 30-day check-in after they had committed to their team agreement. (See chapter 12 for additional context.) They arrived at my office in good spirits. As we walked through each item on their team agreement, it was clear they were functioning more cohesively.

I asked them if there were any adjustments they'd like to make to the team agreement or if they'd like to add anything. Shelly brought up a miscommunication she and Luke had had the week prior about vacation schedules. She had requested time off for a trip she had been planning, and Luke said he had already requested that week off, so she would need to change her plans. Luke had received approval from Danielle for the time off, but Shelly was not aware of Luke's requested time off. To avoid this issue in the future, Shelly asked if they could use their online team calendar to designate requested time off. They all agreed, so we added that to the team agreement. I affirmed them for their clear communication.

With a grin, Shelly looked at Danielle and said that for all their hard work, Danielle owed them lunch. That led to a conversation about how often they connected as a team simply to have fun. From that discussion, they decided to commit to a quarterly lunch and an activity outside of work every six months. We added this to the team agreement as an extra measure of accountability.

Tune-ups like this conversation with Shelly, Luke and Danielle help us slow down and check in. This intentional dialogue causes us to take inventory and reflect. Ultimately, we achieve more of what we want and less of what we don't want in our relationships.

CHAPTER 15

ENJOY A MORE FULFILLING RELATIONSHIP

When Abby walked into my office, I could tell she was on the verge of tears. I invited her to sit down, and she began to tell me her story.

Her co-worker Rachel was her trainer when she came on board six months prior. Abby and Rachel no longer met for regular training, but Abby often went to Rachel's desk to ask her system and procedure questions. In the past month, Rachel had become less and less receptive to Abby's questions. When Abby approached Rachel at her desk, she often didn't even turn to acknowledge Abby's presence. If Abby said, "Excuse me, Rachel. Could

I ask you a question?" Rachel would sometimes snap back with, "I'm busy. Come back later." Abby felt defeated. She was at a loss.

When I asked Abby if she was open to approaching Rachel to resolve this conflict on her own, she said she was not comfortable with that option. I offered to facilitate a conversation between them and asked permission to get Rachel's side of the story. She paused. Then agreed.

When I talked with Rachel, I didn't share Abby's story but simply asked her about the condition of her working relationship with Abby. Rachel told me that Abby constantly interrupted her with questions. Not only did she come to her desk 15 times or more on some days, but she also didn't take notes on the answers so she often asked the same questions over and over. I asked Rachel if she would be open to talking about this with Abby. Rachel agreed.

I told both Rachel and Abby that my role was not to share their stories with each another, but to facilitate a conversation in which they worked out the conflict between them.

I gave each of them the homework of completing the five statements outlined earlier:

1. What I appreciate about you is…
2. What works in our relationship is…
3. What could work better in our relationship is…
4. What I need from you is…
5. Let's brainstorm together ways in which we can work together even better.[1]

When the three of us got together, I first asked them to share what they appreciated about one another. This started the conversation with a deposit in each of their overdrawn emotional bank accounts.

Then I asked them to articulate what they thought could work better in their relationship. Abby shared her frustration with Rachel's lack of response when Abby asked her questions. Rachel shared her stress with Abby's frequent trips to Rachel's desk. They asked curious questions and gained a new awareness of each other's perspective.

They came to the agreement that they would set up two times during the day to meet for questions. Abby committed to holding her questions until these two times in the day when Rachel would answer all of Abby's questions at one time. Rachel offered to help if there was an urgent question that couldn't wait until their designated time, but Abby promised to use that permission sparingly. Abby also agreed to take notes at those Q & A sessions so she could refer back to her notes and avoid asking the same questions over and over. The two of them committed to meet again in 30 days to check in on how their new agreement was working.

I bumped into Rachel in the hallway six months later. She thanked me for that breakthrough conversation. "That conflict resolution stuff really works," she said. "I have to admit that Abby has become one of my best friends at work. That conversation in your office set us on a completely different path. I've discovered I really like her!"

When we do the heavy lifting of a conflict resolution, we get to enjoy the gratification of a more fulfilling relationship. When we see through the other person's eyes and come to a new understanding, we have a new perspective. Like standing on a mountain top, we can see farther and clearer. The view from the Summit is breathtaking.

PUTTING IT ALL TOGETHER

It's time to put all the elements of the model together. Let's go back to the story of Julie rebuilding her trust with her future son-in-law, Jeremy, who had hidden his story of his past drug problem and prison sentence. Julie's daughter, Leah, had forgiven Jeremy, but Julie needed to restore her own trust in Jeremy. (See chapter 6 for additional context.)

Julie used the model to prepare for her conversation with Jeremy. Let's take a look at the steps Julie took.

Step 1—Base Camp: The Preparation

What's at Stake?

Julie needed to consider what was at stake. She was accustomed to a close, transparent relationship with her daughter, Leah. Since the news broke about Jeremy's past, Leah had withdrawn from Julie and the rest of the family. Leah said she had forgiven Jeremy and had resolved the issue with him, although she didn't share how she had come to this resolution. The family was concerned that Leah was getting duped and manipulated by Jeremy. Julie realized that her relationship with Leah was at stake. Leah's future was at stake. And the family's unity was at stake.

What Is Fact and What Is Story?

Julie and her family had heard that Jeremy had used and sold drugs on and off for a year before he was sentenced to prison five years prior. When the news broke shortly after Jeremy and Leah were engaged, they all gathered for a family meeting. At this meeting, Leah's siblings confronted Jeremy with the stories they had heard. Jeremy initially denied the length of time that he had been using and selling drugs. Jeremy claimed that when he got caught, it was the first time he had sold drugs. He later admitted that the time frame he was dealing drugs was, in fact, a year as the family had heard.

Although the family meeting was intended to clear the air and set the record straight, it had the reverse effect. Since Jeremy did not initially admit to the time frame that he had been using and selling drugs, the trust with Leah's family was further damaged. They agreed that Jeremy could not be trusted and that he had been manipulating Leah to believe that he was a man of integrity and worthy to be Leah's husband. Because Leah seemed to move on so quickly after her family confronted Jeremy, they believed Leah was covering her eyes, plugging her ears and pretending the issue didn't exist.

In Base Camp, Julie needed to prepare for her conversation with Jeremy by untangling facts from stories. Here is the list she made:

Facts:
- Jeremy used and dealt drugs for one year.
- At the family meeting, Jeremy denied that he had been dealing drugs for a year.

- Jeremy later confessed that it had been a year.
- Jeremy was convicted and sent to prison.

Story:
- Jeremy could not be trusted.
- Jeremy was manipulating Leah.
- Leah was covering her eyes, plugging her ears and pretending the issue didn't exist.
- Because Jeremy had covered up his past and denied the facts when confronted, he did not deserve to marry Leah.

What Am I Feeling?

Julie was afraid. She was fearful Leah would get hurt. She was afraid Leah would turn her back on the family and walk away with Jeremy. Julie was worried she would lose Leah and Leah would lose herself in her loyalty to Jeremy. Julie was concerned that Leah would be "used up" by her commitment to rehabilitate Jeremy and never pursue her dreams.

What Could Have Been Their Intentions?

Julie struggled to understand why Jeremy would cover up his past and then deny some of the facts once he was confronted. As she spent time in prayer, she came to the realization that Jeremy didn't likely feel safe enough to be transparent. He may have felt it was a greater risk to be honest than to hide. Instead of asking for help when he got into a bad situation, he tried to deal with it on his own. With fear as his guide, the best choice apparent to him when he felt backed into a corner was to cover up the mess he had made. His thinking was not clear, and he was his own worst coach.

When Julie looked through the lens of unconditional love she felt called to, she was able to see Jeremy through the lens of compassion. Julie determined that her role was not to judge Jeremy, but to establish trust. In spite of feeling vulnerable, Julie released her natural desire to control the outcome.

Julie had talked with a friend who insisted that everyone does the best he can at any given moment. Julie said she struggled to believe this applied to Jeremy. She admitted that initially, all she saw in Jeremy was defensiveness and arrogance. But as she reflected and prayed, she came to realize that when Jeremy made the choice to cover up his past, he may have thought he had no other option that would protect his heart and keep him safe.

Julie asked herself, "What would it really cost me to believe in Jeremy? What risk is there in believing he might need mentoring to make better choices in the future?"

Julie knew she would have to set aside her pride and her desire to be right. She would be risking disappointment and possible betrayal again. Jeremy could fail in the future and hurt both Julie and Leah again. But she came to realize that the risk was not as great as the potential loss.

Julie had to wonder if believing in Jeremy could be the bridge of reconciliation. It might also be the inspiration Jeremy needed to launch into his potential. Jeremy may not have been the ideal marriage partner for Leah when they got engaged, but Julie was beginning to acknowledge that perhaps this journey had brought about some maturity and growth in Jeremy. She was softening her heart to the possibility that this experience could have been a refining process that produced new character in Jeremy. Julie was doing her best to stay open to that possibility and to be curious about what change could have transpired in Jeremy's life.

What Part Have I Played?

When Julie reflected on what contribution she had made to the very unsatisfying situation in which she found herself, she realized that she had slipped into a mode of gossip. In her efforts to gain perspective and sort out her feelings as well as the facts, she spent hours talking with her son Andy and other members of the family. She formed her justification for why Jeremy couldn't be trusted and why he was not a suitable husband for her daughter.

She knew she needed to ask Jeremy for forgiveness.

She had drawn a line and stood behind that line expecting Jeremy to come to her and apologize. Julie wanted Leah behind the line to protect her, but Leah broke rank. She sided with Jeremy. Julie came to realize that staying behind the line was not protecting Leah. It was hurting her. Julie loved her daughter deeply. But upon reflection, she asked herself if what she was doing looked like love to Leah. Julie realized that standing behind the line was damaging Julie's relationship with both Leah and Jeremy.

Julie also recognized that she was withholding support and shutting out the possibility that Jeremy could have changed. She believed she needed to ask Jeremy for forgiveness for this. She felt God prompting her to set aside her natural tendency to reject Jeremy if he failed to meet her expectations. She believed God was challenging her to love Jeremy without conditions and without limits.

When she got curious about what God may be doing in Jeremy's life through this situation, she knew she needed to release her desire to control the outcome and leave that in God's hands. She remembered hearing a speaker once say that truth without grace is judgment. She knew she needed God's discernment to strike a balance between the two. She realized that she shouldn't be fighting battles that weren't hers to fight.

What Curious Questions Can I Ask to Create Safety?

Julie determined she would start by getting together with Jeremy and asking curious questions about his background, how he was processing the tension with Leah's family, and how she could support him in his relationship with Leah.

Julie knew she needed to make it safe for Jeremy to be transparent. She wanted to understand his perspective and his concerns. She wanted him to know she cared so she identified a number of curious questions she could ask. They included:

- What was it like to grow up in your home?
- What were your dreams as a child?
- What are your dreams today?
- How has this tension with the family been difficult for you?
- How have you grown as a result of this conflict?
- What has changed in your relationship with Leah?
- What can I do to support you in this journey?
- What does a trusting relationship look like to you?

How Will I Start the Conversation?

By the time Julie had completed her preparation in Base Camp, she had changed. She was determined to set aside her pain and focus on what she felt called to do—love Jeremy unconditionally. She had been earnestly praying for direction, and in the process, her prayer transitioned from "comfort me" to "conform me." She asked God to help her see Jeremy through God's eyes and to listen to his voice. She asked God to help her resist the urge to fix Jeremy, but instead turn over the responsibility for the outcome to God, where it belonged.

Julie had prepared her heart and her one-minute opening statement. She was ready to begin the Ascent.

Step 2—Ascent: The Conversation

Julie and Jeremy met at a restaurant to talk. Jeremy sat nervously as they ordered their meals. He fidgeted with his silverware and looked down at the table frequently.

Julie knew that in order for Jeremy to feel it was safe to be transparent, she needed to let him know that she cared about his concerns and needs. She started with what they had in common—their love for Leah. Julie told Jeremy that she was there because she and Jeremy both shared a deep love for Leah. She told Jeremy that despite the rocky start between him and the family, she wanted what was best for Jeremy and Leah. Julie communicated that she had been praying extensively and that God was calling her to forgive and love Jeremy unconditionally.

As Julie talked, she saw Jeremy relax. He looked her in the eyes instead of down at the table. He stopped fidgeting with his utensils. Julie sensed that Jeremy was beginning to feel safe. She was ready with her opening statement, so they began their Ascent.

State the Issue Without Blame

Jeremy, I want to talk with you about how we can develop a trusting relationship between us.

Give One or Two Examples

As you know, the news about your past drug use and prison sentence hit the family hard. When we confronted you about the issue, and you denied that you had been using and dealing drugs for a year and later admitted it was true, that damaged our trust even further.

Share What Part I've Played

I need to own my part in this issue. I spent more time talking with the other members of the family than I did talking directly with you. I created stories without trying to understand your perspective, and for that, I apologize.

Invite Them to Give Their Perspective

I want to understand how you see this situation, so please share with me how you believe we can develop a trusting relationship.

This opening statement took less than a minute, and it was both respectful and honest. What happened next took Julie by surprise.

Jeremy said he had prepared a statement for Julie too. He said he had written it down in his phone because he wanted to say it just right. Jeremy opened his phone and began reading,

I know that what I did was wrong. The things I did hurt Leah and hurt your family more than I could understand. I had no idea how devastating my actions and my denials would be for so many people. I'm very sorry. You were absolutely right in protecting Leah. I wasn't the kind of man she deserved to marry. I've been working at becoming someone worthy to be Leah's husband, and I've made a lot of changes both emotionally and spiritually. She sees those changes, and we have learned so much from what we've gone through to get this far. She believes in me, and I am very thankful for that. I know I asked for your forgiveness before, but I didn't grasp the extent of my mistakes. So I want to ask again. I know I don't deserve your forgiveness or your trust. I understand that even if you can forgive me, trust needs to be earned, and it will take time. I still want to marry Leah, but whether we get married or not, I want to make things right with your family. I'll do whatever it takes and work for it as long as it takes to regain your trust.

This transparent dialogue penetrated both Julie and Jeremy's hearts, and the trust between them took an exponential leap forward. They connected. Julie asked Jeremy questions about his background and learned that he had been in several foster homes. He struggled with fitting in and measuring up. He seemed to successfully cover up every insecurity and every imperfection—until now. Jeremy came face to face with two competing commitments. He wanted to look perfect—and he wanted to have a trusting relationship with his future in-laws. He had made a big assumption that he would have to make a perfect impression in order to meet the approval of Leah's family.[1] In his determined efforts to gain their approval, he lost the very thing he wanted desperately, their trust.

When Julie created a safe environment for Jeremy, he was free to reflect and learn. In the process, he discovered an oxymoron: the breeding ground for trust is not perfection, but authenticity. It is when we make ourselves vulnerable that people respect us. Even though transparency feels weak on the inside, it demonstrates strength and trustworthiness on the outside.[2]

The dialogue between Julie and Jeremy was rich and transparent. They shifted from being opponents with an issue dividing them to partners determined to solve the problem together. As they talked about building trust between them, trust grew in the process.

Step 3–Summit: The Gratification

Come to an Agreement

Julie and Jeremy agreed to continue working on developing trust in their relationship. They decided that Sunday afternoons would be a good time for Jeremy and Leah to come over for lunch and give both Julie and her husband the opportunity to spend quality time with Jeremy and Leah.

Commit to Action

Julie committed to Jeremy, "I will love you without conditions and without the expectation that you will do what I think you should." Jeremy responded with, "I will be honest and transparent in my relationship with both you and Leah."

Check in for a Tune-Up

After several months of regularly meeting on Sunday afternoons, Julie asked Jeremy to go out for coffee to check in on their agreement to build a trusting relationship. They reflected on the ways their relationship had grown, including laughing together over Sunday lunch and occasional texting throughout the week. Their commitment of time and energy had paid off. They revisited their commitment to action and affirmed each other for the work they had each done to cultivate unconditional love and authenticity.

Enjoy a More Fulfilling Relationship

On the heels of this conflict resolution, Julie described her relationship with Jeremy as a refined trust—a trust that was tested by fire and came through not only restored, but fortified. Because they "went through hell and back," as Julie described it, the relationship between Julie and Jeremy grew beyond what it would have been had they not experienced this conflict.

In this process, Julie reclaimed her relationship with Leah as well. Their tight bond returned. With this opportunity to reset and restart, Julie's connection with Leah catapulted to a new level. Leah's relationship with Jeremy no longer diminished the mother-daughter bond, it augmented it. Julie no longer felt she lost a daughter. Rather, she had gained a son.

With the progress they had made, they were optimistic that over time, the same principles that worked for them would help restore Jeremy's relationship with Andy and the rest of the family as well.

SOME PARTING THOUGHTS

I am indebted to my coaching clients, friends and family who have created the laboratory for this model. I hope the stories that emerged offer inspiration and belief that these principles work. The model of conflict resolution outlined in these pages is simply a set of tools for your toolbox. Because relationships are never static, formulas don't apply.

As you set out to remove a pebble from your shoe and pursue a more fulfilling relationship, pick one conversation—one pebble. Make your preparations in Base Camp. Then look for an opportunity to have the conversation and begin your Ascent. Or simply make an appointment with that person. This commitment on the calendar will get the process in motion.

What would it be like to walk in freedom and have nothing weighing you down in your relationships? It would be liberating. And it's possible. One conversation at a time.

Begin the journey.

The Summit awaits you.

APPENDIX

Step 1—Base Camp: The Preparation

- What's at stake?
- What is fact and what is story?
- What am I feeling?
- What could have been their intentions?
- What part have I played?
- What curious questions can I ask to create safety?
- How will I start the conversation?

Step 2—Ascent: The Conversation

- State the issue without blame
- Give one or two examples
- Share what part I've played
- Invite them to give their perspective

Step 3—Summit: The Gratification

- Come to an agreement
- Commit to action
- Check in for a tune-up
- Enjoy a more fulfilling relationship

NOTES

Introduction

1. Susan Scott, *Fierce Conversations* (New York: Berkley Books, 2004), 254.

Chapter 2—What is Fact and What Is Story?

1. Brené Brown, *Rising Strong: The Reckoning, the Rumble, the Revolution* (New York: Spiegel and Grau, 2015), 37.
2. Ibid., 79.
3. R.A. Burton, *On Being Certain: Believing You Are Right Even When You're Not* (New York: St Martin's Press, 2008), quoted in Brown, 79-80.
4. Thanks to Brené Brown for the inspiration behind the phrase "the story I'm telling myself."

Brené Brown, *Rising Strong: The Reckoning, the Rumble, the Revolution* (New York: Spiegel and Grau, 2015), 86.

Chapter 4—What Could Have Been Their Intentions?

1. Thanks to Senn-Delaney Leadership Consulting Group for the concept of moving from judgment to curiosity.

2. Thanks to Senn-Delaney Leadership Consulting Group for the concept of positive and negative assumptions and their connection to our mood.

Chapter 5—What Part Have I Played?

1. Thanks to Susan Scott for the concept of the silent treatment being toxic to relationships. *Fierce Conversations* (New York: Berkley Books, 2004).

2. Thanks to Susan Scott for the concept of seeing the other person as a partner rather than an opponent. *Fierce Conversations* (New York: Berkley Books, 2004).

Chapter 6—What Curious Questions Can I Ask to Create Safety?

1. "Emotional Safety," *Wikipedia*, https://en.wikipedia.org/wiki/Emotional_safety, accessed July 15, 2016.

2. For more on "lock in" and "lock out," see Larry E. Senn and John R. Childress, *The Secret of a Winning Culture: Building High-Performance Teams* (Los Angeles: The Leadership Press, 1999), 141-142.

Chapter 7—How Will I Start the Conversation?

1. Thanks to Susan Scott for the inspiration behind the concept of a one-minute opening statement. *Fierce Conversations* (New York: Berkley Books, 2004), 148-149.

Chapter 8—State the Issue Without Blame

1. Kerry Patterson, Joseph Grenny, Ron McMillan, Al Switzler, *Crucial Conversations: Tools for Talking When Stakes Are High, 2nd edition* (New York: McGraw-Hill, 2012), 5.

2. Thanks to Susan Scott for the concept that the conversation is about exploration, not combat.

Fierce Conversations (New York: Berkley Books, 2004).

Chapter 12—Come to an Agreement

1. Dennis S. Reina and Michelle L. Reina, *Trust and Betrayal in the Workplace: Building Effective Relationships in Your Organization* (San Francisco: Berrett-Koehler Publishers, Inc., 1999), 96.

2. For more information on public agreements, see Robert Kegan and Lisa Laskow Lahey, *How the Way We Talk Can Change the Way We Work: Seven Languages for Transformation* (San Francisco: Jossey-Bass, 2001).

Chapter 15—Enjoy a More Fulfilling Relationship

1. Dennis S. Reina and Michelle L. Reina, *Trust and Betrayal in the Workplace: Building Effective Relationships in Your Organization* (San Francisco: Berrett-Koehler Publishers, Inc., 1999), 96.

Putting It All Together

1. For more on competing commitments and big assumptions, see Robert Kegan and Lisa Laskow Lahey, *How the Way We Talk Can Change the Way We Work: Seven Languages for Transformation* (San Francisco: Jossey-Bass, 2001).

2. Thanks to Brené Brown for her research on the topic of vulnerability. *Daring Greatly* (New York: Avery, 2012).

ABOUT THE AUTHOR

Linda Outka is a certified coach, speaker and trainer. She is the founder of Breakthrough Solutions, Inc. which creates space where people feel safe to be real and discover new insights that open doors to their potential. Linda is also a founding partner on the John Maxwell Team of coaches, speakers and trainers.

Linda has a Bachelor of Arts in Communication from the University of Northwestern in St. Paul, Minnesota, and a Master of Arts in Human Resource Leadership from Azusa Pacific University in Azusa, California. She also has a number of certifications in team building and coaching instruments.

Connect at LindaOutka.com.

Discover a Breakthrough Solution

Coaching | Conflict Resolution | Team Development

Connect at LindaOutka.com
to receive your free gift.

Creating space where people feel safe to be real
and discover Breakthrough Solutions.

Made in the USA
San Bernardino, CA
08 December 2016